GOING
All
In

Mark Batterson

GOING ALL IN

One Decision Can Change Everything

ZONDERVAN®

ZONDERVAN

Going All In
Copyright © 2013 by Mark Batterson

Requests for information should be addressed to:
Zondervan, *Grand Rapids, Michigan* 49530

ISBN 978-0-310-33787-4

Published in association with the literary agency of Fedd & Company, Inc., Post Office Box 341973, Austin, TX 78734.

Cover design: Extra Credit Projects
Interior design: Beth Shagene

Printed in the United States of America

13 14 15 16 /DPM/ 13 12 11 10 9 8 7 6 5 4 3 2 1

CONTENTS

CHAPTER 1

PACK YOUR COFFIN

A century ago, a band of brave souls became known as one-way missionaries. They purchased single tickets to the mission field without the return half. And instead of suitcases, they packed their few earthly belongings into coffins. As they sailed out of port, they waved good-bye to everyone they loved, everything they knew. They knew they'd never return home.

A. W. Milne was one of those missionaries. He set sail for the New Hebrides in the South Pacific, knowing full well that the headhunters who lived there had martyred every missionary before him. Milne did not fear for his life, because he had already died to himself. His coffin was packed. For thirty-five years, he lived among that tribe and loved them. When he died, tribe members buried him in the middle of their village and inscribed this epitaph on his tombstone:

When he came there was no light.
When he left there was no darkness.

When did we start believing that God wants to send us to safe places to do easy things? That faithfulness is holding the fort? That playing it safe is safe? That there is any greater privilege than sacrifice? That radical is anything but normal?

Jesus didn't die to keep us safe. He died to make us dangerous.

Faithfulness is not holding the fort. It's storming the gates of hell.

The will of God is not an insurance plan. It's a daring plan.

The complete surrender of your life to the cause of Christ isn't radical. It's normal.

It's time to quit living as if the purpose of life is to arrive safely at death.

It's time to go *all in* and *all out* for the *All in All*.

Pack your coffin!

CHAPTER 2

THE INVERTED GOSPEL

In the sixteenth century, the Renaissance astronomer Nicholas Copernicus challenged the belief that the earth was the center of the universe. Copernicus argued that the sun didn't revolve around the earth, but rather that the earth revolved around the sun. The Copernican Revolution turned the scientific world upside down by turning the universe inside out.

In much the same way, each one of us needs to experience our own Copernican Revolution. The paradigm shift happens when we come to terms with the fact that the world doesn't revolve around us. But that's a tough pill to swallow.

When we are born into this world, the world revolves around us. We're spoon-fed on the front end and diaper-changed on the back end. It's as if the entire world exists to meet our every need. And that's fine if you are a two-month-old baby. If you're twenty-two, it's a problem!

Newsflash: *You are not the center of the universe!*

At its core, sinfulness is selfishness. It's enthroning yourself — your desires, your needs, your plans — above all else. You may still seek God, but you don't seek Him first. You seek Him second or third or seventh. You may sing "Jesus at the center of it all," but what you really want is for people to bow down to you as you bow down to Christ. It's a subtle form of selfishness that masquerades as spirituality, but it's not Christ-centric. It's me-centric. It's less about us serving His purposes and more about Him serving our purposes.

I call it the inverted gospel.

Who's Following Who

Most people in most churches think they are following Jesus, but I'm not so sure. They may think they are following Jesus, but the reality is this: *they have invited Jesus to follow them.* They call Him Savior, but they've never surrendered to Him as Lord. And I was one of them. Trust me, I didn't want to go anywhere without Jesus right there behind me. But I wanted Jesus to follow me, to serve my purposes, to do my will.

It wasn't until I was a nineteen-year-old freshman at the University of Chicago that I had my Copernican Revolution. It started with this question: *Lord, what do You want me to do with my life?* That's a dangerous question to ask God, but not nearly as dangerous as *not* asking that question!

I got tired of calling the shots. Honestly, I wasn't very good at playing God. Plus it was exhausting. I stopped trying to "find myself" and decided to seek God. I couldn't read His Word enough. I got up early to pray. I even fasted for the first time in my life. I meant business. In fact, business as usual went out of business. For the first time in my life, I put Him first.

On the last day of summer vacation, I got up at the crack of dawn to do a prayer walk. Our family was vacationing at Lake Ida in Alexandria, Minnesota. The dirt road I walked down may as well have been the road to Emmaus. The cow pasture I walked through may as well have been the back side of the Sinai Desert with a burning bush. After months of asking, I finally got an answer to my question. I knew what God wanted me to do with my life.

On the first day of my sophomore year, I walked into the admissions office at the University of Chicago and told them I was transferring to a Bible college in Springfield, Missouri, to pursue full-time ministry. The guidance counselor thought I was crazy. So did a few friends and family members. Giving up a full-ride scholarship to one of the top-ranked universities in the country didn't make much sense on paper. The logical and practical thing to do would have been to finish my undergrad studies at the U of C and then go to seminary, but I knew this was my all-or-nothing, now-or-never moment. I knew I needed to quit hedging my bets, push all my chips to the middle of the table, and go all in with God.

Was it a gut-wrenching decision? Yes. Did I ever second-guess it? More than once! But the true adventure of following Jesus didn't begin until I went all in. That is the day I stopped asking Jesus to follow me and decided to follow Him.

Let me ask the question: *Who's following who?*

Are you following Jesus?

Or have you inverted the gospel by inviting Jesus to follow you?

Each year, I have the privilege of speaking to tens of thousands of people at churches and conferences all across the country. At first, I was shocked by the response, in a *Christian* audience, to a simple invitation. When I invited people to follow Jesus, about 50 percent would typically respond. What's astounding about that percentage is the simple fact that 100 percent of them thought they were already following Jesus. They weren't. They had inverted the gospel. They bought in, but they hadn't sold out. They were half in and half out.

At first, I thought this was an anomaly. How could half of us get it backward? Now I'm afraid it's normative. And if it is, then we desperately need a new normal.

Holy Dare

More than a hundred years ago, a British revivalist issued a holy dare that would change a life, a city, and a generation. That timeless challenge echoes across every generation: "The world has yet to see what God will do with and for and through and in and by the man who is fully and wholly consecrated to Him."

The original hearer of that call to consecration was D. L. Moody. When those words hit his eardrums, they didn't just fire across synapses and register in his auditory cortex. They shot straight to his soul.

That call to consecration defined his life. And his life, in turn, defined consecration.

It was Moody's all in moment.

Maybe this is yours?

In *The Circle Maker*, the prequel to this book, I wrote about the importance of prayer. It's the difference between the best you can do and the best God can do. You've got to pray a circle around the promises of God the same way the Israelites circled Jericho. And you keep circling until He answers. But you can't just pray like it depends on God. You also have to work like it depends on you. You can't just draw the circle. You also have to draw a line in the sand.

You are only one decision away from a totally different life. Of course, it will probably be the toughest decision you'll ever make. But if you have the courage to completely surrender yourself to the lordship of Jesus Christ, there is no telling what God will do. All bets are off because all bets are on God.

D. L. Moody left an indelible imprint on his generation. In the late 1800s, his sermons contributed to a great spiritual awakening worldwide. And more than a century later, his passion for the gospel continues to indirectly influence millions of people through Moody Church, Moody Bible Institute, and Moody Publishers.

Moody left an amazing legacy, but it all started with a call to consecration. It always does. And nothing has changed. The world has yet to see what God will do with and for and through and in and by the man who is fully and wholly consecrated to Him.

Why not you?
Why not now?

Amazing Things

Anytime God is about to do something amazing in our lives, He calls us to consecrate ourselves to Him. That pattern was established right before the Israelites crossed the Jordan River and conquered the Promised Land.

"Consecrate yourselves, for tomor-

row the Lord will do amazing things among you."

Here's our fundamental problem: *we try to do God's job for Him.* We want to do amazing things for God. And that seems noble, but we've got it backward. God wants to do amazing things for us. That's His job, not ours. Our job is consecration. That's it. And if we do our job, God will most certainly do His.

Before I tell you what consecration is, let me tell you what it isn't.

It's not going to church once a week.

It's not daily devotions.

It's not fasting during Lent.

It's not keeping the Ten
    Commandments.

It's not sharing your faith with friends.

It's not giving God the tithe.

It's not repeating the sinner's prayer.

It's not volunteering for a ministry.

It's not leading a small group.

It's not raising your hands in worship.

It's not going on a mission trip.

All of those things are good things,

but that isn't consecration. It's more than behavior modification. It's more than conformity to a moral code. It's more than doing good deeds. It's something deeper, something truer.

The word *consecrate* means to *set yourself apart*. By definition, consecration demands *full devotion*. It's dethroning yourself and enthroning Jesus Christ. It's the complete divestiture of all self-interest. It's giving God veto power. It's surrendering *all of you* to *all of Him*. It's a simple recognition that every second of time, every ounce of energy, and every penny of money is a gift *from* God and *for* God. Consecration is an ever-deepening love for Jesus, a childlike trust in the heavenly Father, and a blind obedience to the Holy Spirit. Consecration is all that and a thousand things more. But for the sake of simplicity, let me give you my personal definition of consecration.

Consecration is going *all in* and *all out* for the *All in All*.

All In

My greatest concern as a pastor is that people can go to church every week of their lives and never go *all in* with Jesus Christ. They can follow the rules but never follow Christ. I'm afraid we've cheapened the gospel by allowing people to buy in without selling out. We've made it too convenient, too comfortable. We've given people just enough Jesus to be bored but not enough to feel the surge of holy adrenaline that courses through your veins when you decide to follow Him no matter what, no matter where, no matter when.

The Danish philosopher and theologian Søren Kierkegaard believed that boredom was the root of all evil. In other words, boredom isn't just boring. It's wrong. You cannot be in the presence of God and be bored at the same time. For that matter, you cannot be in the will of God and be bored at the same time. If you follow in the footsteps of Jesus, it will be anything but boring.

The choice is yours — consecration or

boredom? It's one or the other. If you don't consecrate yourself to Christ, you'll get bored. If you do, you won't. And that is where the battle is won or lost. If you don't go all in, you'll never enter the Promised Land. But if you go all out, God will part the Jordan River so you can cross through on dry ground.

Stop trying to do God's job for Him. You don't have to do amazing things. You can't do amazing things. *Amazing always begins with consecration*. It's the catalyst behind every spiritual growth spurt, every kingdom cause, and every revival. And just as amazing always begins with consecration, *consecration always ends with amazing*.

When you look back on your life, the greatest moments will be the moments when you went all in. It's as true today as it was the day Abraham placed Isaac on the altar, the day Jonathan climbed a cliff to fight the Philistines, and the day Peter got out of the boat and walked on water.

In the pages that follow, we'll look at a dozen all in moments that double as defining moments in Scripture. I'll also share stories of ordinary people who are making an extraordinary difference with their lives. They will inspire you to risk more, sacrifice more, and dream more.

The longer I follow Jesus, the more convinced I am of this simple truth: God doesn't do what God does *because of* us. God does what God does *in spite of* us. All you have to do is stay out of the way.

It's that simple. It's that difficult.

Stay humble. Stay hungry.

If you aren't hungry for God, you are full of yourself. That's why God cannot fill you with His Spirit. But if you will empty yourself, if you will die to self, you'll be a different person by the time you reach the last page of this book. As I wrote this book, I prayed that God would rewrite your life. It starts with giving the Author and Perfecter of your faith full editorial control. If you let go and let God take control, He'll write history, His Story, through your life.

CHAPTER 3

DRAW THE LINE

"Take up your cross daily,
and follow me."
Luke 9:23 NLT

In AD 44, King Herod ordered that James the Greater be thrust through with a sword. He was the first of the apostles to be martyred. And so the bloodbath began. Luke was hung by the neck from an olive tree in Greece. Doubting Thomas was pierced with a pine spear, tortured with red-hot plates, and burned alive in India. In AD 54, the proconsul of Hierapolis had Philip tortured and crucified because his wife converted to Christianity while listening to Philip preach. Philip continued to preach while on the cross. Matthew was stabbed in the back in Ethiopia. Bartholomew was flogged to death in Armenia. James the Just was thrown off the southeast pinnacle of the temple in Jerusalem. After surviving the one-hundred-foot fall, he was clubbed to death by a mob. Simon the Zealot was crucified by a governor of Syria in AD 74. Judas Thaddeus was beaten to death with sticks in Mesopotamia. Matthias, who replaced Judas Iscariot, was stoned to death and then beheaded. And Peter was crucified upside down at his own request. John the Beloved is the only disciple to die of natural causes, but that's only because he survived his own execution. When a cauldron of boiling oil could not kill John, Emperor Diocletian exiled him to the island of Patmos, where he lived until his death in AD 95.

Every Christian living in a first-world country in the twenty-first century should read *Foxe's Book of Martyrs*. It's a reality check that puts our first-world problems into perspective. It redefines risk and sets the standard for sacrifice. By comparison, many of our risks seem rather tame and many of our sacrifices seem somewhat lame.

Our normal is so subnormal that normal seems radical. To the first-century disciples, *normal* and *radical* were synonyms. We've turned them into antonyms.

In Luke 9:23 – 24, Jesus threw down the gauntlet with his disciples. He wanted to see who was in and who was out. Or more accurately, who was *all in*.

> *"Whoever wants to be my disciple must deny themselves and take up their cross daily and follow me. For whoever wants to save their life will lose it, but whoever loses their life for me will save it."*

The disciples took this literally. We can at least take it figuratively. I'm not suggesting we *will* die physically for Christ, but we *must* die to ourselves. If Jesus hung on His cross, we can certainly carry ours! And that isn't just our greatest responsibility. It's our highest privilege.

Anything less than the complete surrender of our lives to the lordship of Jesus

Christ is robbing God of the glory He demands and deserves. It's also cheating ourselves out of the eternal reward God has reserved for us.

We won't come alive, in the truest and fullest sense, until we die to self. And we won't find ourselves until we lose ourselves in the cause of Christ.

It's time to ante up.

It's time to go all in.

If Jesus is not Lord *of all*, then Jesus is not Lord *at all*.

It's all or nothing.

It's now or never.

The Americanized Gospel

We have Americanized the gospel or spiritualized the American Dream. Take your pick. But neither one comes close to the true gospel. When you try to add something to the gospel, you aren't enhancing it. Any addition is really a subtraction. The gospel, in its purest form, is as good as it gets.

We want God on our terms, but we

don't get God that way. That's how we get false religion. It's pick and choose. It's cut and paste. The end result is a false god we've created in our image.

You only get a relationship with God on His terms. You can take it or leave it, but you cannot change the rules of engagement. And you don't want to!

The apostle Paul defines the deal that is on the table this way:

> God made him who had no sin to be sin for us, so that in him we might become the righteousness of God.

The moment you bow your knee to the lordship of Jesus Christ, all of your sin is transferred to Christ's account and paid in full. It was nailed to the cross two thousand years ago! But that's only half the gospel. Mercy is *not* getting what you deserve — the wrath of God. Grace is getting what you *don't* deserve — the righteousness of Christ. Everything you've done wrong is forgiven and forgotten. And everything Christ did right — His righteousness — is transferred to your account. And then God calls it even.

It's like God says, "I'll take the blame for everything you did wrong and give you credit for everything I did right." It doesn't get any better than that, and that's why it's called the gospel. It's not just good news. It's the best news.

The gospel costs nothing. We cannot buy it or earn it. It can only be received as a free gift, compliments of God's grace. So it costs nothing, but it demands every-thing. And that is where most of us get stuck — spiritual no-man's-land. We're too Christian to enjoy sin and too sinful to enjoy Christ. We've got just enough Jesus to be informed, but not enough to be transformed.

We want everything God has to offer without giving anything up. We want to buy in without selling out. We're afraid that if we don't hold out on God, we'll miss out on what this life has to offer. It's a lie. It's the same lie the serpent told Adam and Eve in the garden. God is not holding out on you.

You can take Psalm 84:11 to the bank:

No good thing does God withhold from those who walk uprightly.

If you don't hold out on God, I can promise you this: God will not hold out on you. But it's all or nothing.

It's *all of you* for *all of Him*.

No Sacrifice

Let me put my cards on the table.

I don't think anyone has ever sacrificed anything for God. If you get back more than you gave up, have you sacrificed anything at all? The eternal reward always outweighs the temporal sacrifice. At the end of the day, Judgment Day, our only regret will be whatever we didn't give back to God.

This may seem counterintuitive, but I'm convinced it's true: the key to self-fulfillment is self-denial. Self-denial is shorthand for delayed gratification. And by delay, I don't mean days or months or years. I mean a lifetime. Our delayed gratification on earth translates into eternal glory in heaven.

The selfish part of us has an allergic reaction to the word *deny*. It's tough to do when we live in the lap of luxury. We don't just tolerate indulgence in our culture. We celebrate it. But the fundamental problem with indulgence is that *enough is never enough*. The more we indulge ourselves in food or sex or the amenities of wealth, the less we will enjoy them. It's not until we go *all in* with God that we discover that true joy is only found on the sacrificial side of life.

I cannot prove this quantitatively, but I know it's true: *the more you give away, the more you will enjoy what you have*. If you give God the tithe, you'll enjoy the 90 percent you keep 10 percent more. You'll also discover that God can do more with 90 percent than you can do with 100 percent. If you double tithe, you'll enjoy the 80 percent you keep 20 percent more! One of our life goals as a family is to reverse tithe and live off 10 percent while giving away 90 percent. When we get there, I'm confident we'll enjoy the 10 percent we keep 90 percent more. It's the sliding scale of joy.

Most of us spend most of our lives accumulating the wrong things. We've bought into the consumerist lie that *more is more*. We mistakenly think that the more we give, the less we'll have. But in God's upside-down economy, our logic is backward. You ultimately lose whatever you keep and you ultimately keep whatever you lose for the cause of Christ.

I think of a little rhyme that doubled as a playground rule when I was a kid: *finders keepers, losers weepers*. It's the exact opposite in God's kingdom: *finders weepers, losers keepers*.

The Rich Young Ruler

On paper, the Rich Young Ruler was the epitome of religiosity. But religiosity and hypocrisy are kissing cousins. In reality, the Rich Young Ruler is the antitype of all in. And his life is a standing warning: *if we hold out on God, we'll miss out on everything God wants to do in us, for us, and through us.* Of course, the flip side is true as well.

I haven't met many people possessed by a demon, but I've met a lot of people possessed by their possessions. They don't own things. Things own them. And that is certainly true of the Rich Young Ruler. He had everything money could buy. He had his whole life in front of him. And he called his own shots. Yet something was missing. The emptiness in his soul was evidenced by the question he asked Jesus:

What am I still missing?

The Rich Young Ruler had everything we think we want. He was rich. He was young. And he was in a position of power. What more could he possibly want? What could he possibly be missing? And why was he so miserable? The answer is easy: he was *following the rules*, but he wasn't *following Jesus*. And I think that is true of far too many people in far too many churches.

The Rich Young Ruler may rank as one of the most religious people in the pages of

Scripture. The text tells us he kept *all* the commandments. He did nothing wrong, but you can do nothing wrong and still do nothing right. By definition, righteousness is doing something right. We've reduced it to doing nothing wrong.

We fixate on sins of commission: *Don't do this, don't do that — and you're OK.* But that is holiness by subtraction. And it's more hypocrisy than holiness! It's the sins of omission — what you would have, could have, and should have done — that break the heart of your heavenly Father. How do I know this? Because I'm an earthly father! I love it when my kids don't do something wrong, but I love it even more when they do something right.

The heavenly Father is preparing good works in advance with our name on them. He is ordering our footsteps. And He is able to do immeasurably more than all we can ask or imagine. But we can't just play defense. We have to play offense! We can't just do nothing wrong. We have to do something right. We can't just follow the rules. We have to follow Jesus.

The story of the Rich Young Ruler is one of the saddest stories in the Bible because he had so much upside potential. He could have leveraged his resources, his network, and his energy for kingdom causes, but he spent it all on himself. He thought that was what would make him happy, but that was what made him miserable. It reveals that our *greatest asset* becomes our *greatest liability* if we don't use it for God's purposes!

The Rich Young Ruler eventually became the Old Rich Ruler. I don't know what fired across his synapses as he lay on his deathbed, but I have a hunch. It was the moment Jesus said, "Follow me." Those words echoed in his ear until the day he died. It was the opportunity of a lifetime, but he didn't have the guts to go for it. He held his hand instead of doubling down on Jesus.

The importance of going all in is best encapsulated in the parable of the bags of gold. The man who got one bag buried it in the ground. He ultimately gave back to the master exactly what the master had given him. And to be perfectly honest, that's not half bad in a recession. He broke even. Yet Jesus called him *wicked*.

That seems like a little bit of an overreaction, doesn't it? In fact, I'd be tempted to play Peter and pull Jesus aside and tell Him to dial it back just a bit. But when I think Jesus is wrong, it reveals something wrong with me — usually a wrong priority or a wrong perspective. It means I'm missing the point. The man who buried his bag of gold wasn't willing to gamble on God. He didn't even ante up. And that's the point of this parable: faith is pushing all of your chips to the middle of the table. You can't hedge your bet by setting aside one or two chips. It's all or nothing. And that's what Jesus challenged the Rich Young Ruler to do.

> *"If you want to be perfect, go, sell your possessions and give to the poor, and you will have treasure in heaven. Then come, follow me."*

Accumulate Experiences

Be honest, have you ever felt bad for the Rich Young Ruler? Part of me feels like Jesus was asking for too much. *Are You sure You want to ask for everything? Why don't You start with the tithe*? But Jesus goes for the jugular. He asks the Rich Young Ruler to ante up everything. Why? Because He loved the Rich Young Ruler too much to ask for anything less!

We focus on what Jesus asked him to *give up* but fail to consider what He *offered up* in exchange. Jesus invited the Rich Young Ruler to follow Him. And that's the point in the story where we should *gasp*.

I live in the internship capital of the world. Tens of thousands of twentysomethings flock to the nation's capital every summer because the right internship with the right person can open the right door. It's all about building your résumé. I daresay that no one in the history of humankind has ever been offered a better internship opportunity than the Rich

Young Ruler. An internship with the Creator of the heavens and the earth? Come on, that's gotta look good on a job application. What a reference! And the Rich Young Ruler said *no*.

So if you feel bad for the Rich Young Ruler, it shouldn't be because of what Jesus asked him to give up. It should be because of the opportunity he passed up. What Jesus asked him to give up was nothing compared to what Jesus would have given him in return. The Rich Young Ruler had everything money could buy, but it was all worthless compared to the priceless experiences he could have had following Jesus.

In a day and age when the average person never traveled outside a thirty-mile radius of their home, Jesus sent His disciples to the ends of the earth. These uneducated fishermen, who would have lived their entire lives within a stone's throw of the Sea of Galilee, traveled all over the ancient world and turned it upside down.

Think about their experiences during their three-year internship with Jesus.

They went camping, hiking, fishing, and sailing with the Son of God. They had box seats to every sermon Jesus preached and then hung out with Him backstage. They didn't just witness His miracles. They filleted the miraculous catch of fish, fried it, and ate it. Put that on your bucket list. What kind of price tag would you put on walking on water? Or drinking the water that Jesus turned into wine?

The disciples were poor in terms of material possessions, but they accumulated a wealth of experience unparalleled in human history. The Rich Young Ruler forfeited a wealth of experience because he couldn't let go of his possessions.

Don't accumulate possessions. Accumulate experiences!

Senior Partner

I have a ninety-five-year-old friend named Stanley Tam. More than a half century ago, Stanley made a defining decision to go all in with God. In one of the most unique corporate takeovers ever, Stanley legally transferred 51 percent of the shares of his company to God. It took three lawyers to pull it off, because the first two thought he was crazy!

Stanley started the United States Plastic Corporation with $37 in capital. When he gave his business back to God, annual revenues were less than $200,000. But Stanley believed God would bless his business, and he wanted to honor God from the get-go.

At that point, most of us would have been patting ourselves on the back. Not Stanley. He felt convicted for keeping 49 percent for himself. After reading the parable about the merchant who sold everything to obtain the pearl of great price, Stanley made a decision to divest himself of all his shares.

I love Stanley's plainspoken words: "A man can eat only one meal at a time, wear only one suit of clothes at a time, drive only one car at a time. All this I have. Isn't that enough?"

On January 15, 1955, every share of stock was transferred to his Senior Partner, and Stanley became a salaried employee of the company he had started. That is the day Stanley went *all in* with God. From that day to the present, Stanley has given away more than $120 million!

I love telling Stanley's story because he's a hero of mine. I also think it's where the rubber meets the road. You can tell me you're all in, but let me see your calendar and your credit card statement. They don't lie. How we spend our time and our money are the two best barometers of our true priorities.

Is Jesus Christ your Pearl of Great Price?

Is He your Senior Partner?

Draw the Line

Destiny is not a mystery. It's a decision. And you are only one decision away from a totally different life. One decision can totally change your financial forecast. One decision can radically alter a relationship. One decision can lead toward health — spiritual, physical, or emotional. And those defining decisions will become the defining moments of your life.

For Stanley Tam, the defining moment was January 15, 1955.

For me, it was the first day of my sophomore year of college. And there have been a half dozen defining decisions since then. The day we packed all of our earthly belongings into a U-Haul truck and moved to Washington, DC, with no guaranteed salary and no place to live. The day National Community Church decided to launch its second location without knowing where it would be. The day Lora and I made a faith promise to missions that was way beyond our budget.

Those defining decisions proved to be defining moments. You only make a few defining decisions in your life, but they will define your life.

What risk do you need to take?

What sacrifice do you need to make?

This isn't a book to read. It is a decision to be made. If you read this book without making a defining decision, I wasted my time writing it and you wasted your time reading it. At some point, on some page, you will feel the Holy Spirit prompting you to act decisively. Don't ignore it. Obey it.

In *The Circle Maker*, I wrote about the importance of prayer. It's the difference between the best you can do and the best God can do. You've got to circle the promises of God in prayer the way the Israelites circled the city of Jericho. But you can't just draw the circle. You also need to draw a line in the sand.

You need to put Isaac on the altar like Abraham.

You need to throw down your staff like Moses.

You need to burn your plowing equipment like Elisha.

You need to climb the cliff like Jonathan.

You need to get out of the boat like Peter.

There comes a moment when you throw caution to the wind.

There comes a moment when you need to go *all in*.

There comes a moment when you need to burn the ships.

This is that moment.
This is your moment.
It's all or nothing.
It's now or never.

NOTES

Chapter 2: The Inverted Gospel

Page 20: *The world has yet to see*: Quoted in William R. Moody, *The Life of Dwight L. Moody* (New York: Revell, 1900), 134; see Mark Fackler, "The World Has Yet to See …," *Christianity Today* (January 1, 1990), www.ctlibrary.com/ch/1990/issue25/2510.html (accessed February 11, 2013).

Page 22: *Consecrate yourselves*: Joshua 3:5.

Chapter 3: Draw the Line

Page 31: *In AD 44, King Herod ordered*: James's martyrdom is the only one mentioned in Scripture. See Acts 12:1 – 2.

Page 31: *And so the bloodbath began*: See Grant R. Jeffrey, *The Signature of God* (Frontier Research, 1996), 254 – 57.

Page 35: *God made him who had no sin*:
   2 Corinthians 5:21.

Page 37: *No good thing does God*: Psalm 84:11 ESV.

Page 39: *the Rich Young Ruler*: Luke 18:18–30.

Page 40: *What am I still missing?* Matthew 19:20
   CEB.

Page 42: *parable of the bags of gold*: Matthew
   25:14–30.

Page 43: *If you want to be perfect*: Matthew 19:21.

All In

You Are One
Decision Away
from a Totally
Different Life

Mark Batterson,
New York Times
bestselling author

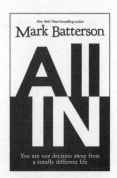

Halfway is no way to live! Quit holding back. Quit holding out. It's time to go all in and all out for God.

If Jesus hung on His cross for us, the least we can do is carry our cross for Him. And the good news is this: If you don't hold out on God, God won't hold out on you. In reality, no one has ever truly sacrificed anything for God because the eternal reward always outweighs the temporal discomfort.

Many people believe they are following Jesus, but they have mistakenly invited Jesus to follow them. Mark Batterson calls it the inverted gospel. In *All In*, he challenges you to fully surrender your life to the lordship of Jesus Christ. That is when the true adventure begins.

The Circle Maker

Praying Circles Around Your Biggest Dreams and Greatest Fears

Mark Batterson

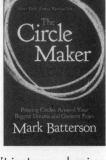

According to Pastor Mark Batterson, "Drawing prayer circles around our dreams isn't just a mechanism whereby we accomplish great things for God. It's a mechanism whereby God accomplishes great things in us."

Do you ever sense that there is far more to prayer and to God's vision for your life than what you're experiencing? It's time you learned from the legend of Honi the circle maker — a man bold enough to draw a circle in the sand and not budge from inside it until God answered his prayers for his people.

What impossibly big dream is God calling you to draw a prayer circle around? Sharing inspiring stories from his own experiences as a circle maker, Mark Batterson will help you uncover your heart's deepest desires and God-given dreams and unleash them through the kind of audacious prayer that God delights to answer.

The Circle Maker Video Curriculum

Praying Circles Around Your Biggest Dreams and Greatest Fears

Mark Batterson

This dynamic video curriculum helps participants understand what it means to dream God-sized dreams, pray with boldness, and think long-term. Four video sessions combine a teaching element from Mark Batterson with a creative element to draw viewers into the circle. Each session wraps up with a practical application giving the opportunity to put prayer principles into practice. Available as a pack, which includes one softcover participant's guide and one DVD. Participant guides are also sold separately.

Session titles include:

1. Becoming a Circle Maker
2. Little People, Big Risks, and Huge Circles
3. Praying Hard and Praying Through
4. Praying Is Like Planting

Also available: Curriculum Kit, which includes one hardcover book, one participant's guide, one DVD-ROM containing four small-group video sessions, a getting-started guide, four sermon outlines, and all the church promotional materials needed to successfully launch and sustain a four-week church-wide campaign. The curriculum can also be used in adult Sunday school settings, for small group studies, and for individual use.

The Circle Maker, Student Edition

Dream Big, Pray Hard, Think Long.

Mark Batterson
with Parker Batterson

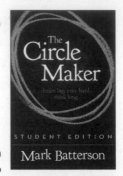

Prayer can sometimes be a frightening thing: How do you approach the Maker of the world, and what exactly can you pray for? In this student adaptation of *The Circle Maker*, Pastor Mark Batterson uses the true legend of Honi the circle maker, a first-century Jewish sage whose bold prayer saved a generation, to uncover the boldness God asks of us at times, and to unpack what powerful prayer can mean in your life. Drawing inspiration from his own experiences as a circle maker, as well as sharing stories of young people who have experienced God's blessings, Batterson explores how you can approach God in a new way by drawing prayer circles around your dreams, your problems, and, most importantly, God's promises. In the process, you'll discover this simple yet life-changing truth:

> *God honors bold prayers and*
> *bold prayers honor God.*

And you're never too young for God to use you for amazing things.

Draw the Circle

The 40 Day Prayer Challenge

Mark Batterson

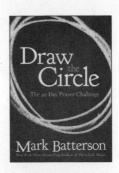

Do you pray as often and as boldly as you want to? There is a way to experience a deeper, more passionate, persistent, and intimate prayer life.

In this forty-day devotional, Mark Batterson applies the principles of his *New York Times* bestselling book *The Circle Maker* to teach you a new way to pray. As thousands of readers quickly became many tens of thousands, true stories of miraculous and inspiring answers to prayer began to pour in. These testimonies will light your faith on fire and help you pray with even more boldness.

In *Draw the Circle*, through forty true, faith-building stories of God's answers to prayers, daily Scriptures, and prayer prompts, Batterson inspires you to pray and keep praying like never before.

Begin a lifetime of watching God work. Believe in the God who can do all things. Experience the power of bold prayer and even bolder faith in *Draw the Circle*.

ZONDERVAN®
.com

Praying Circles around Your Children

Mark Batterson

In this 112-page booklet, Mark Batterson shares a perfect blend of biblical yet practical advice that will revolutionize your prayer life by giving you a new vocabulary and a new methodology. You'll see how prayer is your secret weapon. Through stories of parents just like you, Batterson shares five prayer circles that will not only help you pray for your kids, but also pray through your kids.

Batterson teaches about how to create prayer lists unique to your family, claim God-inspired promises for your children, turn your family circle into a prayer circle, and discover your child's life themes. And he not only tells you how, he illustrates why.

As Batterson says, "I realize that not everyone inherited a prayer legacy like I did, but you can leave a legacy for generations to come. Your prayers have the power to shape the destiny of your children and your children's children. It's time to start circling."

The Circle Maker Prayer Journal

Mark Batterson

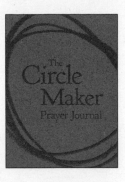

Discover the power of bold prayer and even bolder faith in God's promises. Based on Mark Batterson's revolutionary, bestselling book on prayer, *The Circle Maker Prayer Journal* features inspirational sayings and plenty of space to record your prayers, God's answers, and your spiritual insights. Learn to pray powerful words according to God's will — and see the amazing results! Gather your prayers so you can go back and see how God has been answering since you started your amazing prayer journey.

The Circle Maker Prayer Journal will be your guide to making your life goals a reality of answered prayers instead of merely fleeting wishes. This handsomely bound keepsake volume will become your written record for dreaming big and seeing God's answers.

ZONDERVAN®
.com

Find Mark online at www.markbatterson.com,
on Facebook at www.facebook.com/markbatterson,
and on Twitter @MarkBatterson.